Music for Little Mozarts

A Piano Course to Bring Out the Music in Every Young Child

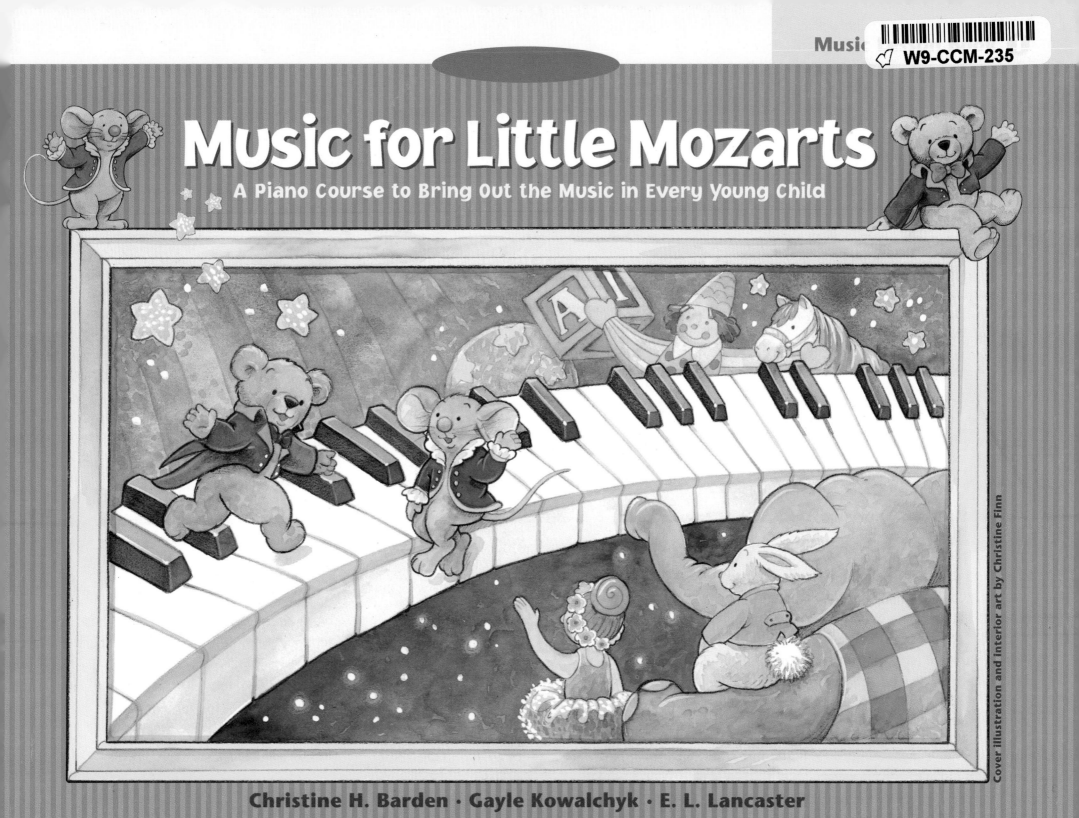

Cover illustration and interior art by Christine Finn

Christine H. Barden · Gayle Kowalchyk · E. L. Lancaster

ISBN 0-88284-966-2

Foreword

Recent studies suggest that playing and listening to music at a young age improves learning, memory, reasoning ability and general creativity. Research also supports the theory that young children who are exposed to music develop enhanced cognitive skills. The *Music for Little Mozarts* series was written to provide appropriate piano instruction for four-, five- and six-year-olds while simultaneously developing listening skills. The series was designed to provide a balance between the discipline necessary for playing the instrument and the enjoyment one gets from the process of music-making.

The course centers around the adventures of Beethoven Bear and Mozart Mouse as they learn about music. Three books guide the children through a comprehensive approach to musical learning. In the *Music Lesson Book*, students are introduced to new musical concepts and performance of pieces at the piano as they follow the story of Beethoven Bear and Mozart Mouse. Plush animals of the two characters are integral to making the course fun for young students. The *Music Workbook* contains carefully designed pages to color, that reinforce the musical concepts introduced in the Music Lesson Book. In addition, well-planned listening activities develop ear-training skills. The *Music Discovery Book* contains songs that allow the students to experience music through singing, movement and response to rhythm patterns. Music appreciation is fostered through carefully chosen music that introduces the students to great music through the ages. Melodies to sing, using either solfege or letter names, help students learn to match pitch and discover tonal elements of music. Correlated compact disc recordings for materials in the Music Lesson and Music Discovery Books are essential to achieve the goals of the course. General MIDI disks also are available for students or teachers who have the necessary equipment. A Starter Kit includes a music bag for carrying lesson materials, a music activity board and the two plush animal characters (Beethoven Bear and Mozart Mouse).

Role of Parents: The teacher serves as a musical guide for young students in fostering their curiosity, natural ability and interest, but parents also play an important role in guiding their child's musical training. The authors recommend that parents attend lessons with their child and participate actively in the learning process. Parents will need to read the directions to their child during daily practice. Regularity of practice is important; short practice sessions of 10–15 minutes are suggested for young students, with activities changing frequently within the practice time. (Teachers can give valuable suggestions regarding practice.) Patience, sincere praise and a show of enthusiasm about new materials will be very beneficial. A musical partnership between parents and child in a nurturing environment provides quality time for fostering important family relationships.

Notes to the Teacher: The course is easy to use both in private and group lessons. Through careful pacing and reinforcement, appealing music with clever lyrics is introduced in the Music Lesson Book. The Music Workbook and Music Discovery Books are correlated page by page with the Music Lesson Book to provide well-balanced lessons. A separate Teacher's Handbook offers suggestions and lesson plans to aid the teacher with planning.

All books contain clean and uncluttered pages, clear music engraving and attractive artwork to complement the music and appeal to young children.

About the Music Lesson Book 1: The Music Lesson Book is the core of the course. The story of Beethoven Bear and Mozart Mouse sets the stage for music study at the beginning and continues on each subsequent page. New concepts are introduced and carefully reinforced throughout the book. Each page contains a fragment of the story as background for each new concept or new piece of music, as well as practice instructions to read to the student. Many pages also give helpful hints to the teacher and parents for effective instruction and practice. Numbers for these hints correspond to numbers in the practice directions for the student. The music was written to develop finger dexterity in young children and includes clever lyrics that will appeal to the student's imagination. Accompaniments for the teacher or parent are notated for each piece. The CD includes the narration of the story as well as performances of the pieces with orchestrated accompaniments. Each example on the CD is identified by an icon followed by the track number. Likewise, each example on the GM disk is identified by an icon, followed by the Type 0 file number and the Type 1 file number (in parentheses).

The authors and publisher of this course offer our best wishes to children, parents and teachers as you begin this new adventure. It is certain to be richly rewarding!

Contents

Beethoven Bear and Mozart Mouse and the Musical Argument

Once upon a time, there was a large house where a family with children just about your age lived. In that house, there was a wonderful playroom filled with every kind of toy imaginable. There were dolls and books, trains and trucks, puzzles and crayons and even a trunk with clothes for playing make believe. The children who lived in the house loved playing in this room. But of all the toys they had, their favorite ones were a little stuffed bear and a little stuffed mouse. Their names were Beethoven Bear and Mozart Mouse.

Everyone knows that children play with toys. But do you know what toys do when children are not around? They play too! All of the toys played with one another in the playroom when the family was not at home. Well… all of them, that is, except Beethoven Bear and Mozart Mouse. When the family was away, they would sneak out of the playroom to their favorite place in the house—the Music Room!

Beethoven Bear and Mozart Mouse thought that the Music Room was the most special place in the whole house. It had shelves from floor to ceiling filled with music and books about music. There were cozy chairs and a sofa where the family sat as the children performed.

But the very best thing in the whole room according to the little bear and mouse was the piano. They could not wait to hop on the keys and make beautiful sounds.

When the house was empty (except for the toys, of course!), Beethoven Bear and Mozart Mouse would creep out of the playroom and go to their favorite spot, the Music Room.

As they hurried down the stairs, Beethoven Bear would sometimes say to Mozart Mouse, "I can't wait to play some low sounds!"

Mozart Mouse would reply, "I like high sounds the best!"

"No!" Beethoven Bear would argue. "Low sounds are best. They are perfect for a bear like me."

"No!" Mozart Mouse would reply. "The high sounds are perfect for a mouse like me."

And so went the argument that Beethoven Bear and Mozart Mouse had many times when they played in the Music Room.

When they weren't arguing, they would take a peek in the big book that was always left open on the music rack of the piano. "This must be a Magical Music Book," said Beethoven Bear. Mozart Mouse added, "It is simply wonderful! We can learn so many things from this book."

You can help Beethoven Bear and Mozart Mouse discover many exciting things about music by following the pages through the *Music for Little Mozarts* series. Let your musical adventure begin so you can share your favorite sounds with Beethoven Bear, Mozart Mouse, your friends and your family.

How to Sit at the Piano and Curve Your Fingers!

The first time Beethoven Bear and Mozart Mouse hid in the Music Room, they watched the children practice. They were trying to get ideas of things that they could do when they had a chance to get at the piano themselves!

"See how the children sit at the piano?" Beethoven Bear whispered excitedly. "They . . .

- Sit tall!

- Let their arms hang loosely from their shoulders.

- Place the bench facing the piano squarely.

- Keep their knees slightly under the keyboard.

"Since I'm small myself, I will sit on a book or cushion like the smallest children!" Mozart Mouse remarked.

"Look! If the children's feet don't touch the floor, they place a book or stool under their feet," they both recited together.

"And most importantly, the children *always* play with curved fingers."

"One more thing, though," Beethoven Bear said, giggling, "They never, *never* eat honey or cheese at the piano!"

1. Practice holding your hand pretending that you have a bubble in your hand.

2. Hold the bubble gently, so that it doesn't pop.

Low Sounds

🔢 3

The next time they entered the Music Room, Beethoven Bear ran to the piano bench first. He climbed up and sat on the left side of the bench.

"Oh, I do *so* like playing LOW sounds!" he said, knowing that LOW sounds are on the LEFT side of the keyboard.

1 Place Beethoven Bear on the side of the keyboard (left) that makes LOW sounds.

2 Find LOW sounds on your keyboard using BOTH hands. Play all 10 fingers at once on any low keys (cluster). Play LOW sounds on each word as you say:

"My bear likes LOW sounds."

🔢 4

3 Now find and play LOW sounds (cluster) with your LEFT hand as you say:

"My bear likes LOW sounds."

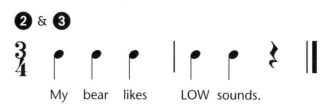

────── **Teacher and Parent** ──────

Say the words in this rhythm and keep a steady beat. Students can find any low keys.

2 & **3**

My   bear   likes   LOW   sounds.

High Sounds

🔵5

Mozart Mouse followed quickly and joined Beethoven Bear on the bench.

"I have *always* preferred music that uses HIGH sounds. I find them quite refreshing!" argued Mozart Mouse, remembering that HIGH sounds are on the RIGHT side of the keyboard.

1 Place Mozart Mouse on the side of the keyboard (right) that makes HIGH sounds.

2 Find HIGH sounds on your keyboard using BOTH hands. Play all 10 fingers at once on any high keys (cluster). Play HIGH sounds on each word as you say:

"My mouse likes HIGH sounds!"

🔵6

3 Now find and play HIGH sounds (cluster) with your RIGHT hand as you say:

"My mouse likes HIGH sounds!"

──────── Teacher and Parent ────────

Say the words in this rhythm and keep a steady beat. Students can find any high keys.

2 & **3**

My mouse likes   HIGH sounds.

$\frac{3}{4}$

Moving Up the Keyboard

🎵7

After playing low sounds for a while, Beethoven Bear decided he wanted a change.

By starting LOW on the keyboard and moving UP (to the right), he made HIGHER sounds—just like the sounds his friend Mozart Mouse made.

① Place Beethoven Bear on the low end of the keyboard and walk him UP the keys to the high end.

② Play LOW sounds on your keyboard using EITHER hand. Continue playing sounds that move up (to the right) until you hear HIGH sounds.

🎵8

③ Your teacher will show you how to slide your hand up the keyboard (glissando). Using your RIGHT hand, start LOW on the keyboard and play a glissando moving up until you hear HIGH sounds.

UP (High Sounds) ➡️ **RIGHT**

──────── **Teacher and Parent** ────────

To make the activities on this page easier, students may stand and move to the right as they play.

Moving Down
the Keyboard

🎵9

not to be outdone, Mozart Mouse wanted a change, too. He saw that by starting HIGH on the keyboard and moving DOWN (to the left), he could make LOWER sounds.

"Hmmm," he thought to himself. "I might not want to *say* so, but I think I like these low sounds almost as much as Beethoven Bear does!"

1 Place Mozart Mouse on the high end of the keyboard and walk him DOWN the keys to the low end.

2 Play HIGH sounds on your keyboard using EITHER hand. Continue playing sounds that move down (to the left) until you hear LOW sounds.

🎵10

3 Using your LEFT hand, start HIGH on the keyboard and play a glissando moving down until you hear LOW sounds.

LEFT ⬅ **DOWN** (Low Sounds)

————— Teacher and Parent —————

To make the activities on this page easier, students may stand and move to the left as they play.

Loud Sounds

🔊11

In the Magical Music Book on the piano, Beethoven Bear discovered the musical name for LOUD: *forte*.

He shouted: "I can play *forte* anywhere on the keyboard!"

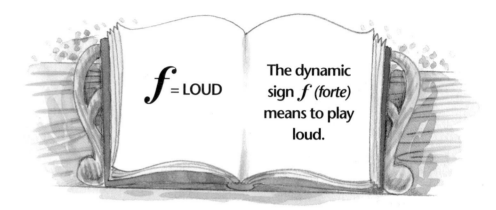

f = LOUD

The dynamic sign f (forte) means to play loud.

🔊12

1 Place Beethoven Bear on the LOW end of the keyboard. Using BOTH of your hands, play LOUD (f) sounds LOW on the keyboard.*

2 Place Beethoven Bear in the MIDDLE of the keyboard. Using BOTH of your hands, play LOUD (f) sounds in the MIDDLE of the keyboard.*

3 Place Beethoven Bear on the HIGH end of the keyboard. Using BOTH of your hands, play LOUD (f) sounds HIGH on the keyboard.*

*Play LOUD sounds on each word using all 10 fingers at once (cluster) as you say:

"My bear plays LOUD sounds!"

—————— Teacher and Parent ——————

Say the words in this rhythm and keep a steady beat as the student plays LOUD sounds.

Soft Sounds

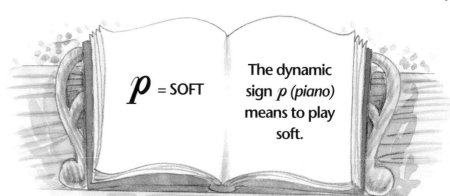

p = SOFT

The dynamic sign p (piano) means to play soft.

🔊13

Turning the page, Mozart Mouse showed Beethoven Bear the musical name for SOFT sounds: *piano.* "Soft sounds are quiet and peaceful," he whispered.

"And I can play SOFT sounds anywhere on the keyboard," he whispered even more quietly.

🔊14

1 Place Mozart Mouse on the HIGH end of the keyboard. Using EITHER of your hands, play SOFT (p) sounds HIGH on the keyboard.*

2 Place Mozart Mouse in the MIDDLE of the keyboard. Using EITHER of your hands, play SOFT (p) sounds in the MIDDLE of the keyboard.*

3 Place Mozart Mouse on the LOW end of the keyboard. Using EITHER of your hands, play SOFT (p) sounds LOW on the keyboard.*

* Play SOFT sounds on each word using all 5 fingers at once (cluster) as you say:

"My mouse plays SOFT sounds."

————— Teacher and Parent —————

Say the words in this rhythm and keep a steady beat as the student plays SOFT sounds.

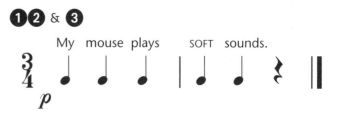

Left Hand
Finger Numbers

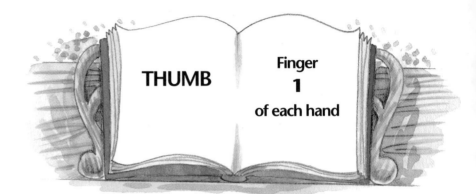

THUMB is **Finger 1** of each hand

🎵15

Beethoven Bear wanted to use his left hand to play low sounds. But he wasn't sure which fingers he should use.

"Look!" said Mozart Mouse. "The Magical Music Book says that the THUMB is the first finger of each hand."

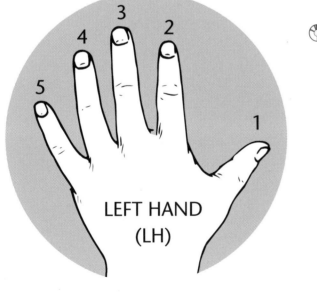

LEFT HAND (LH)

🎵16

1 Hold up your LEFT HAND and show Beethoven Bear how to:

- Wiggle finger 1 (Thumbkin)
- Wiggle finger 2 (Pointer)
- Wiggle finger 3 (Tall Man)
- Wiggle finger 4 (Ring Man)
- Wiggle finger 5 (Pinky)

2 Draw an outline of your LEFT HAND in the space above.

3 Number each finger of the outline.

―――――――――― **Teacher and Parent** ――――――――――

1 Name some left-hand fingers for the student to wiggle.

2 Help the student draw an outline of his/her LEFT HAND (LH) in the space above.

3 Help the student number each finger of the outline.

Right Hand Finger Numbers

🔊17

"Learning the *right*-hand finger numbers should be easy now," said Mozart Mouse.

"Yes," said Beethoven Bear. "Just remember that the thumb is the first finger of the right hand, too."

────── **Teacher and Parent** ──────

1 Name some right-hand fingers for the student to wiggle.

2 Help the student draw an outline of his/her RIGHT HAND (RH) in the space above.

3 Help the student number each finger of the outline.

🔊18

1 Hold up your RIGHT HAND and show Mozart Mouse how to:

- Wiggle finger 1 (Thumbkin)
- Wiggle finger 2 (Pointer)
- Wiggle finger 3 (Tall Man)
- Wiggle finger 4 (Ring Man)
- Wiggle finger 5 (Pinky)

2 Draw an outline of your RIGHT HAND in the space above.

3 Number each finger of the outline.

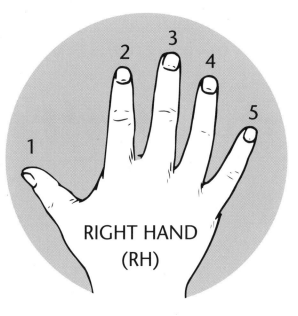

RIGHT HAND (RH)

2 Black Keys

🔘19

Beethoven Bear noticed that the keyboard is made up of black keys and white keys. He then discovered that black keys are found in groups of **2** and groups of **3**.

He said to Mozart Mouse, "Let's see if we can find and play groups of **2** black keys!"

Mozart Mouse thought that was a grand idea and so he agreed.

🔘20

1 Place Beethoven Bear on 2 LOW black keys. Using LH fingers 2 and 3, play 2 black keys LOW on the keyboard (both keys at once). Play 2 low black keys loudly (f) on each word as you say:

"My bear plays 2 LOW black keys."

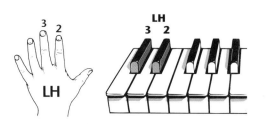

2 Place Mozart Mouse on 2 HIGH black keys. Using RH fingers 2 and 3, play 2 black keys HIGH on the keyboard (both keys at once). Play 2 high black keys softly (p) on each word as you say:

"My mouse plays 2 HIGH black keys."

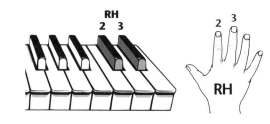

3 Using fingers 2 and 3 of either hand, play ALL the 2 black key groups on the entire keyboard.

---Teacher and Parent---

Say the words in this rhythm and keep a steady beat as the student plays 2 black keys (both keys at once).

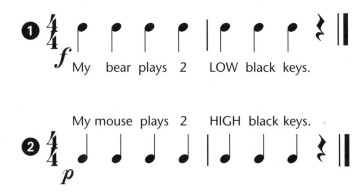

Quarter Note

🔵21

"**W**hat should we *do* with the 2 black key groups?" Mozart Mouse asked. "Let's play quarter notes on them!" suggested Beethoven Bear. "I learned about them in the Magical Music Book."

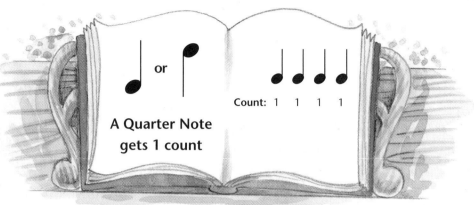

or

A Quarter Note gets 1 count

Count: 1 1 1 1

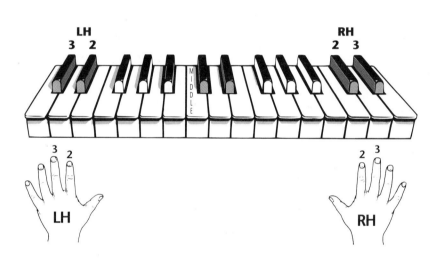

🔵22

1 Using LH fingers 2 and 3, play quarter notes on 2 black keys near the middle of the keyboard (both keys at once). Play two times. First count aloud and then say the words.

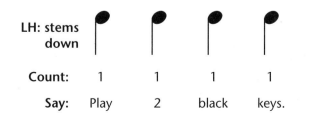

LH: stems down			
Count: 1	1	1	1
Say: Play	2	black	keys.

2 Using RH fingers 2 and 3, play quarter notes on 2 black keys near the middle of the keyboard (both keys at once). Play two times. First count aloud and then say the words.

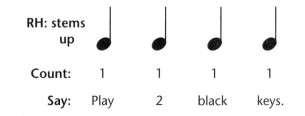

RH: stems up			
Count: 1	1	1	1
Say: Play	2	black	keys.

Bar Lines

🔘23

After reading about bar lines in the Magical Music Book, Beethoven Bear climbed on the keyboard and started "walking in place" on 2 black keys. He thought about how bar lines would help him keep his place in the music, and began to hum a tune to himself. . . .

1 Place Beethoven Bear on 2 black keys.

2 Clap (or tap) *Left Hand Walking* and count aloud evenly.

3 Point to the quarter notes below and count aloud evenly.

4 Say the finger numbers aloud while playing them in the air.

5 Play one key at a time and say the finger numbers.

6 Play and sing the words.

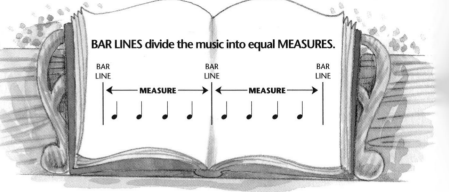

BAR LINES divide the music into equal MEASURES.

Left Hand Walking

🔘24 MIDI 1 (26)

DOUBLE BAR
used at
the end.

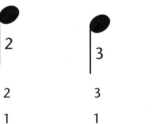

Sing:	Left	hand	walk	- ing,				
Count:	1	1	1	1	1	1	1	1

Student plays two times with duet part.

🔊25

"Step, right, step, right!" interrupted Mozart Mouse as he marched on the 2 black keys.

"If only my friends from the toyroom would join in my parade," he shouted.

1. Place Mozart Mouse on 2 black keys.
2. Clap (or tap) *Right Hand Marching* and count aloud evenly.
3. Point to the quarter notes below and count aloud evenly.
4. Say the finger numbers aloud while playing them in the air.
5. Play one key at a time and say the finger numbers.
6. Play and sing the words.

Right Hand Marching

🔊26 🎹2(27)

Sing: Right hand march - ing,   2   3   2   3
Count: 1   1   1   1   1   1   1   1

Student plays two times with duet part.

March tempo

Teacher or Parent

mf

1.   2.

8va

3 Black Keys

🔊27

"**W**hat about the **3** black key groups?" Mozart Mouse asked Beethoven Bear.

"Oh, yes!" said Beethoven Bear, remembering that black keys are found in groups of **2** *and* in groups of **3**.

"Now let's see if we can find and play groups of **3** black keys!"

🔊28

1 Place Beethoven Bear on 3 LOW black keys. Using LH fingers 2, 3 and 4, play 3 black keys LOW on the keyboard (all keys at once). Play 3 low black keys loudly (f) on each word as you say:

"My bear plays 3 LOW black keys."

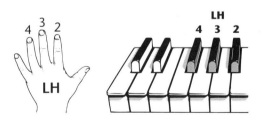

2 Place Mozart Mouse on 3 HIGH black keys. Using RH fingers 2, 3 and 4, play 3 black keys HIGH on the keyboard (all keys at once). Play 3 high black keys softly (p) on each word as you say:

"My mouse plays 3 HIGH black keys."

3 Using fingers 2, 3 and 4 of either hand, play ALL the 3 black key groups on the entire keyboard.

—————— **Teacher and Parent** ——————

Say the words in this rhythm and keep a steady beat as the student plays 3 black keys (all keys at once).

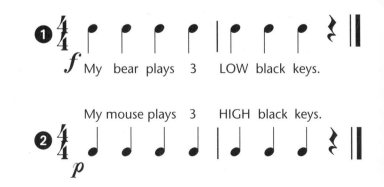

Quarter Rest

🔊 29

"I am quite tired," puffed Mozart Mouse.

"Why don't we rest for the length of one quarter rest?" suggested Beethoven Bear.

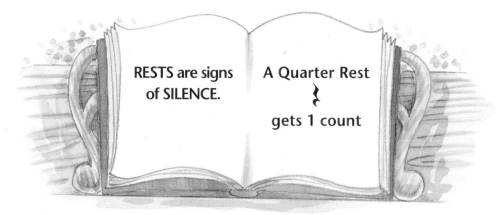

RESTS are signs of SILENCE.

A Quarter Rest 𝄽 gets 1 count

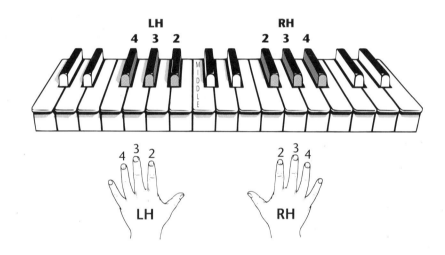

🔊 30

1 Using LH fingers 2, 3 and 4, play the following rhythm on 3 black keys near the middle of the keyboard (all keys at once). Play two times. First count aloud (whisper REST on the 𝄽) and then say the words.

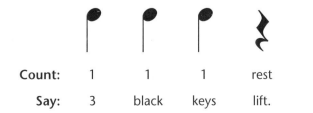

Count:	1	1	1	rest
Say:	3	black	keys	lift.

2 Using RH fingers 2, 3 and 4, play the following rhythm on 3 black keys near the middle of the keyboard (all keys at once). Play two times. First count aloud (whisper REST on the 𝄽) and then say the words.

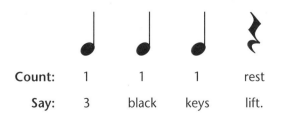

Count:	1	1	1	rest
Say:	3	black	keys	lift.

🎵31

*"L*isten, Mozart Mouse, listen!" Beethoven Bear had written a song for the left hand using the 3 black keys and was *ever* so eager to play it.

1 Place Beethoven Bear on 3 black keys.

2 Clap (or tap) *A Bear's Song* and count aloud evenly.

3 Point to the quarter notes and rests below and count aloud evenly.

4 Say the finger numbers aloud while playing them in the air.

5 Play one key at a time and say the finger numbers.

6 Play and say the words.

A Bear's Song

🎵32 💾3(28)

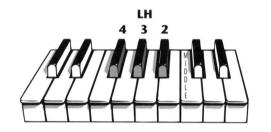

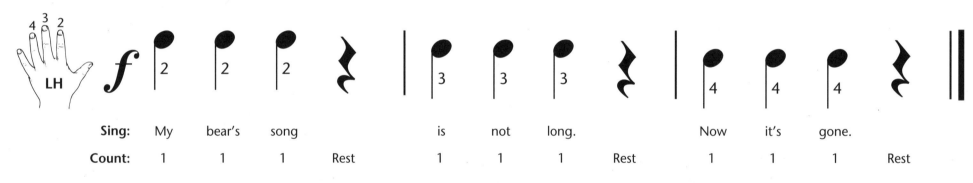

Sing:	My	bear's	song		is	not	long.		Now	it's	gone.	
Count:	1	1	1	Rest	1	1	1	Rest	1	1	1	Rest

Student plays one octave higher with duet part.

Brightly

Teacher or Parent

🔵33

After hearing Beethoven Bear's new song, Mozart Mouse was inspired to compose a new song for himself.

1. Place Mozart Mouse on 3 black keys.
2. Clap (or tap) *A Mouse's Melody* and count aloud evenly.
3. Point to the quarter notes and rests below and count aloud evenly.
4. Say the finger numbers aloud while playing them in the air.
5. Play one key at a time and say the finger numbers.
6. Play and say the words.

A Mouse's Melody

🔵34 💾4(29)

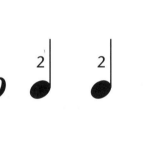

Sing:	Moz	- art	Mouse		plays	and	then		runs	a	- way.	
Count:	1	1	1	Rest	1	1	1	Rest	1	1	1	Rest

Student plays one octave lower with duet part.

Delicately

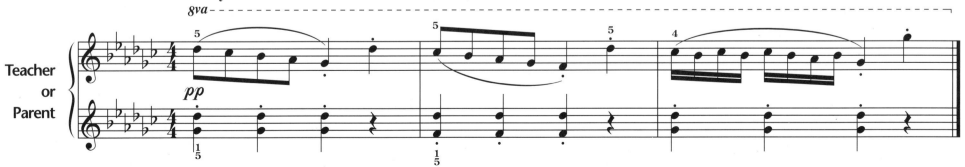

⊙35

It occurred to Beethoven Bear and Mozart Mouse that they had already learned a lot!

"Look, Beethoven Bear," Mozart Mouse exclaimed, "I think we now know how to play the song that we sing about our farm friends!"

1. Sing the words *Old MacDonald had a farm*, then clap (or tap) *E - I - E - I - O* evenly as you sing.

2. Clap (or tap) *E - I - E - I - O* and count aloud evenly.

3. Point to the quarter notes and rests below and count aloud evenly.

4. Say the finger numbers aloud while playing them in the air.

5. Play *E - I - E - I - O* and say the finger numbers.

6. Sing the words *Old MacDonald had a farm* (2nd time: *On that farm he had a duck*) and play *E - I - E - I - O*.

E- I - E - I - O!

⊙36 MIDI 5 (30)

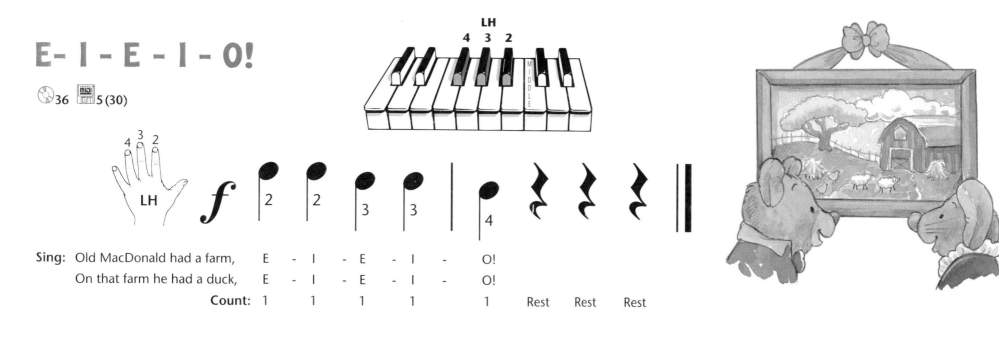

Sing: Old MacDonald had a farm,   E - I - E - I - O!
       On that farm he had a duck,   E - I - E - I - O!
Count: 1   1   1   1   1   Rest   Rest   Rest

Student plays two octaves higher with duet part. (Student plays two times.)

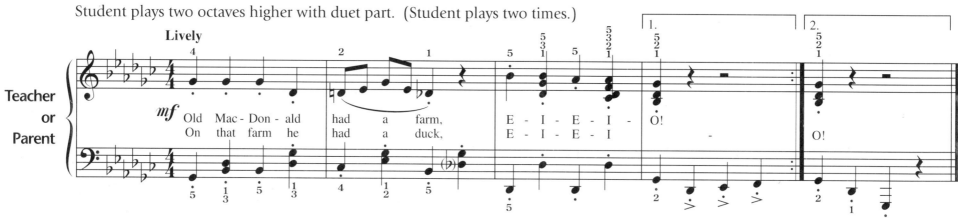

Teacher or Parent

mf Old Mac-Don-ald had a farm, E - I - E - I - O!
     On   that farm he   had a duck, E - I - E - I - O!

37 "Oh, let's see . . . what else is on Old MacDonald's farm?" pondered Mozart Mouse.

"The ponies—remember the ponies!" Beethoven Bear replied.

1 Sing the words *Going for a pony ride,* then clap (or tap) *On MacDonald's Farm* evenly as you sing.

2 Clap (or tap) *On MacDonald's Farm* and count aloud evenly.

3 Point to the quarter notes and rests below and count aloud evenly.

4 Say the finger numbers aloud while playing them in the air.

5 Play *On MacDonald's Farm* and say the finger numbers.

6 Sing the words *Going for a pony ride* (2nd time: *Music friends ride side by side*) and play *On MacDonald's Farm.*

On MacDonald's Farm

38 6 (31)

Sing:	Going for a pony ride	On	Mac	- Don -	ald's	Farm.			
	Music friends ride side by side	On	Mac	- Don -	ald's	Farm.			
Count:	1	1	1	1		1	Rest	Rest	Rest

Student plays one octave higher with duet part. (Student plays two times.)

🔴39

On MacDonald's farm, Beethoven Bear and Mozart Mouse sometimes took turns riding the pony.

But truly, both of them had the most fun when they rode the pony *together*.

① Place Beethoven Bear on 3 black keys and Mozart Mouse on 2 black keys.

② Clap (or tap) *Rockin' Pony Ride* and count aloud evenly.

③ Point to the quarter notes and rests below and count aloud evenly.

④ Say the finger numbers aloud while playing them in the air.

⑤ Play using LH & RH and say the finger numbers.

⑥ Play and sing the words.

Rockin' Pony Ride

🔴40 💾7 (32)

Repeat Sign:
2 DOTS mean go back to the beginning and play again.

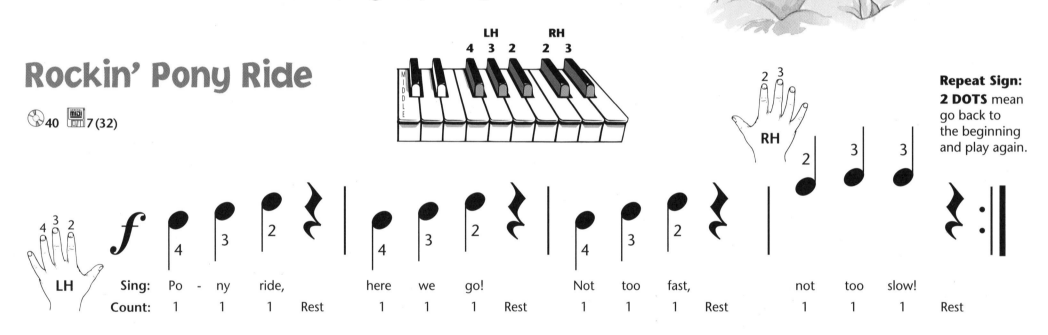

🔘 41

"**W**hoa! Whoa!" cried Beethoven Bear, still pretending to ride the pony. "Can we play *Rockin' Pony Ride* in the opposite direction, starting with the right hand? We could call it *Down We Go*."

Mozart Mouse replied, "What a clever idea! And we could slow down—I'm a bit out of breath!"

1 Place Beethoven Bear on 2 black keys and Mozart Mouse on 3 black keys.

2 Clap (or tap) *Down We Go* and count aloud evenly.

3 Point to the quarter notes and rests below and count aloud evenly.

4 Say the finger numbers aloud while playing them in the air.

5 Play using RH & LH and say the finger numbers.

6 Play and sing the words.

Down We Go

🔘 42 💾 8 (33)

Sing:	Down	we	go,		in	a	row.		This	song	goes		high	to	low.	
Count:	1	1	1	Rest	1	1	1	Rest	1	1	1	Rest	1	1	1	Rest

Student plays one octave higher with duet part.

Slow blues tempo

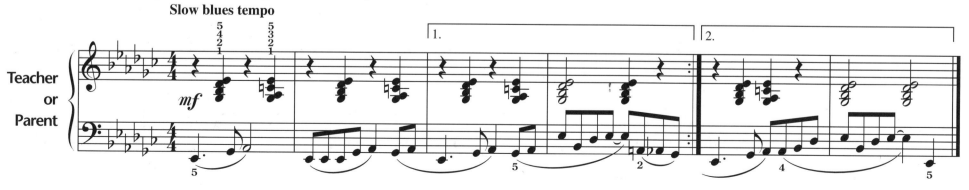

Teacher or Parent

mf

Finding D
on the Keyboard

🔘43

After playing many black keys, it was time for Beethoven Bear and Mozart Mouse to play white keys. They knew that piano keys were named for the first seven letters of the alphabet: A, B, C, D, E, F, G.

"Hey, let's find the D key!" announced Beethoven Bear courageously, looking in the Magical Music Book.

"D is the white key between the two black keys."

1 Find each D on the keyboard below and color it YELLOW.

2 Place Beethoven Bear on your piano, touching a D.

3 Play every D on your piano keyboard.

🔊44 "At last! Our first white key!" Beethoven Bear shouted excitedly.

"Look, Beethoven Bear, we can play a song using D!" Mozart Mouse added.

1 Clap (or tap) *The D Song* and count aloud evenly.

2 Point to the quarter notes & rests below and count aloud evenly.

3 Using RH finger 2, play and sing the words.

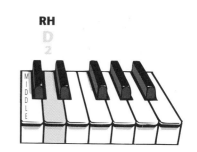

The D Song

🔊45 🎹9 (34)

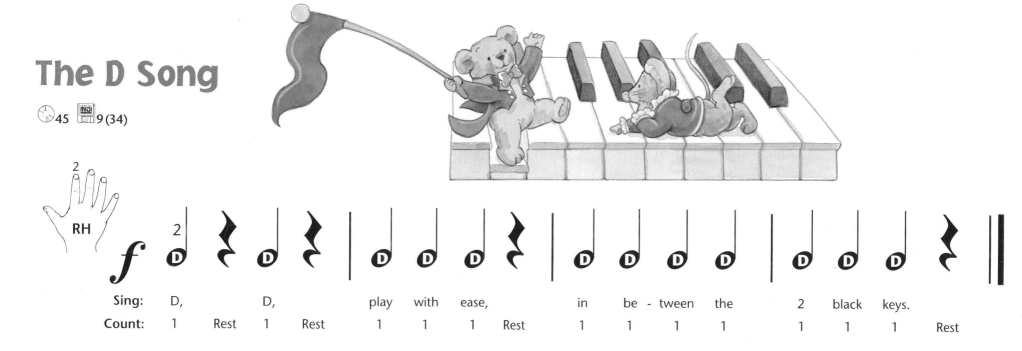

Student plays one octave higher with duet part.

Finding C
on the Keyboard

🎵46

no sooner had they played their new key, when they discovered a second key, C.

"C is the white key to the LEFT of the two black keys!" said Mozart Mouse, pointing to the Magical Music Book.

1 Find each C on the keyboard below and color it GREEN.

2 Place Mozart Mouse on your piano, touching a C.

3 Play every C on your piano keyboard.

🔘47

"We have learned two keys. One for you and one for me!" exclaimed Beethoven Bear.

"Now we can practice playing this new key that we have learned," Mozart Mouse said.

1. Clap (or tap) *The C Song* and count aloud evenly.

2. Point to the quarter notes & rests below and count aloud evenly.

3. Using RH finger 1, play and sing the words.

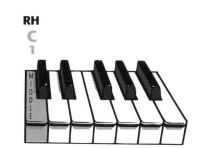

The C Song

🔘48 💾10(35)

Sing: C,   C,   if you please,   just be - low the   2 black keys.

Student plays one octave higher with duet part.

Moving along

Teacher or Parent

🔘49

After learning two white keys, Mozart Mouse immediately wanted to compose a *minuet*.

"It runs in my family," he proudly informed Beethoven Bear. "The Mouse family has *always* enjoyed a good minuet!"

"I would love to hear it!" responded Beethoven Bear. "May I dance?" he asked.

1 Clap (or tap) *Mozart Mouse's First Minuet* and count aloud evenly.

2 Point to the quarter notes & rests below and count aloud evenly.

3 Say the finger numbers aloud while playing them in the air.

4 Play and say the finger numbers.

5 Play and say the note names.

6 Play and sing the words.

Mozart Mouse's First Minuet

🔘50 💾11 (36)

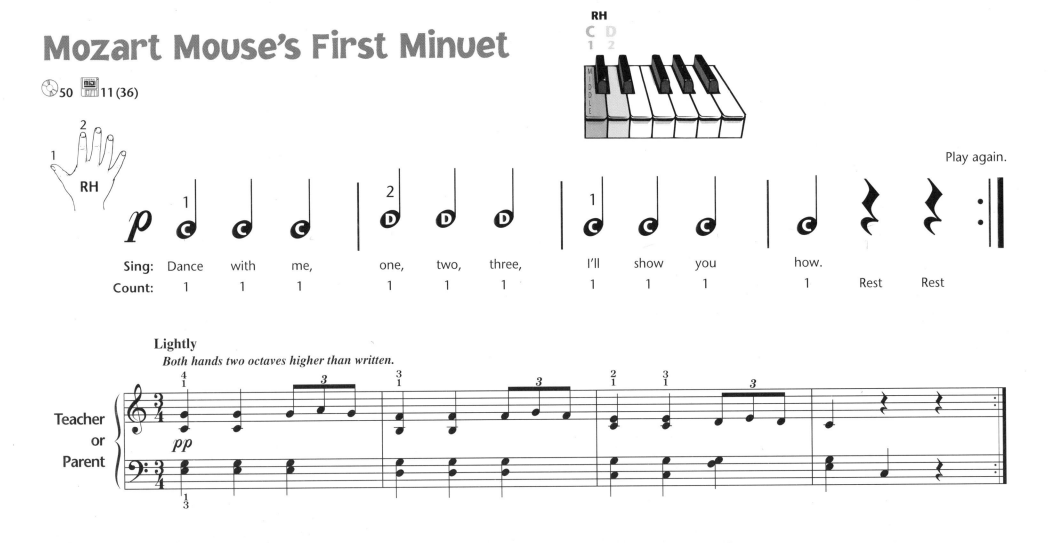

| Sing: | Dance | with | me, | one, | two, | three, | I'll | show | you | how. | Rest | Rest |
| Count: | 1 | 1 | 1 | 1 | 1 | 1 | 1 | 1 | 1 | 1 | | |

Lightly
Both hands two octaves higher than written.

Teacher
or
Parent

Half Note

🕐51

Looking once again into the Magical Music Book, Mozart Mouse learned about half notes.

"... hmm, let's see..." he murmured, deep in thought. "A half note gets TWO counts."

Beethoven Bear, however, quietly and quite unnoticed, closed his eyes and fell fast asleep.

1 Clap (or tap) *Nap Time* and count aloud evenly.

2 Point to the half notes & quarter rests below and count aloud evenly.

3 Say the finger numbers aloud while playing them in the air.

4 Play and say the finger numbers.

5 Play and say the note names.

6 Play and sing the words.

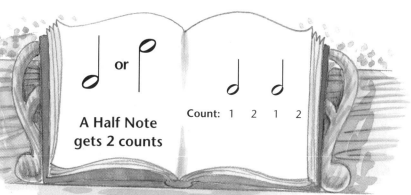

A Half Note gets 2 counts

Count: 1 2 1 2

Nap Time

🕐52 🎹12(37)

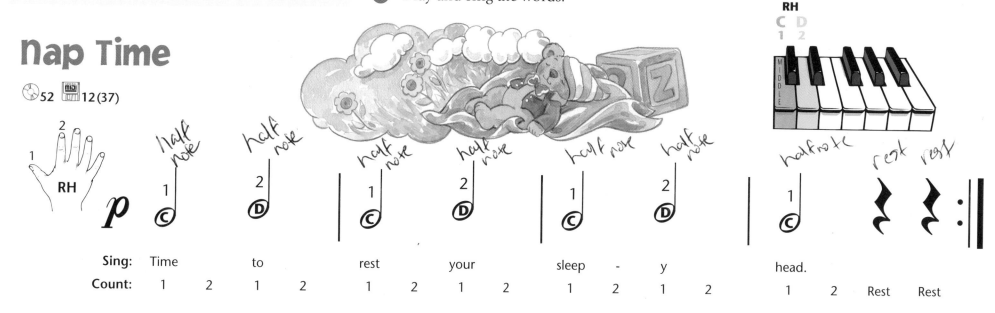

Sing:	Time		to		rest		your		sleep	-	y		head.			
Count:	1	2	1	2	1	2	1	2	1	2	1	2	1	2	Rest	Rest

Student plays one octave higher with duet part.

Slow lullaby

Teacher or Parent

Finding E on the Keyboard

🎵53

"**W**ake up! Wake up!" Mozart Mouse insisted.

"Remember when we first learned about D? Then we discovered C?"

Mozart Mouse eagerly continued, "Well, I think we have found the E key! E is the white key to the RIGHT of the two black keys."

1. Find each E on the keyboard below and color it RED.

2. Place Mozart Mouse on your piano, touching an E.

3. Play every E on your piano keyboard.

🔘54

"E is the *highest* key we've learned so far!" Beethoven Bear realized.

"Very observant, my friend!" Mozart Mouse said politely, although he was already beginning to play *The E Song*.

1. Clap (or tap) *The E Song* and count aloud evenly.

2. Point to the quarter notes & rests below and count aloud evenly.

3. Using RH finger 3, play and sing the words.

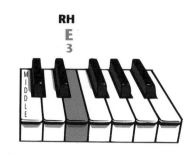

The E Song

🔘55 MIDI 13 (38)

Sing: E, E, look for me. I'm a - bove the 2 black keys.

Student plays one octave lower with duet part.

Gently

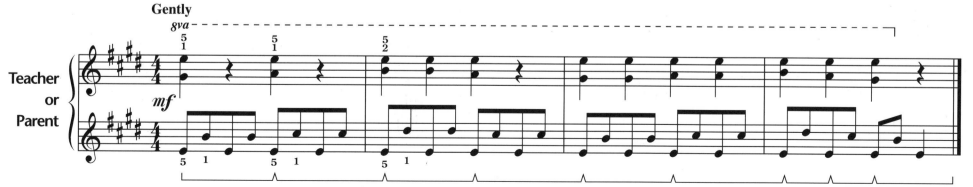

Teacher or Parent

34

🔘56

"Now what are you playing?" the ever-curious Beethoven Bear inquired, noticing that Mozart Mouse was playing a different song.

Mozart Mouse replied, "It is a *Music Friend Waltz* for you! After all, you *are* my best friend!" He then continued happily playing, glad that Beethoven Bear was his friend and that they now knew *three* keys!

1. Clap (or tap) *Music Friend Waltz* and count aloud evenly.
2. Point to the notes & rests below and count aloud evenly.
3. Say the finger numbers aloud while playing them in the air.
4. Play and say the finger numbers.
5. Play and say the note names.
6. Play and sing the words.

Music Friend Waltz

🔘57 MIDI 14(39)

Sing: Waltz with me, one, two, three, Now take a bow.

Student plays one octave higher with duet part.

Moderate waltz tempo

Teacher or Parent

Half Rest

🔊 58

"I want to write a symphony, I want to play a masterpiece!" Beethoven Bear was getting very excited.

"A masterpiece?... well... I don't know," Mozart Mouse responded. "But why don't you write a *three-note* symphony? And you could use half rests like we found in the Magical Music Book!"

1 Clap (or tap) *A Three-Note Symphony* and count aloud evenly.

2 Point to the half notes & half rests below and count aloud evenly.

3 Say the finger numbers aloud while playing them in the air.

4 Play and say the finger numbers.

5 Play and say the note names.

6 Play and sing the words.

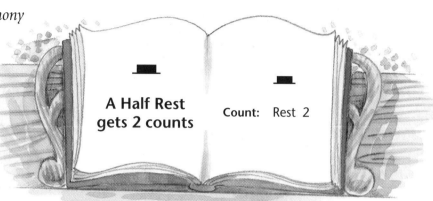

A Half Rest gets 2 counts   Count: Rest 2

A Three-Note Symphony

🔊 59 💾 15 (40)

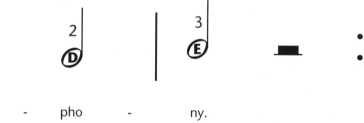

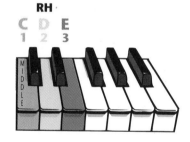

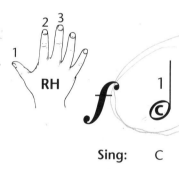   

Sing:	C	D	E		Sym	-	pho	-	ny.	
Count:	1	2	1	2	1	2	Rest	2	1	2	1	2	1	2	Rest	2

Slow and steady

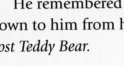**60**

Beethoven Bear immediately wanted to write a variation of his new song. It had a melody quite similar to a song he once knew.

He remembered an old folk tale, handed down to him from his grandmother, about a *Lost Teddy Bear*.

1. Clap (or tap) *Lost Teddy Bear* and count aloud evenly.
2. Point to the half notes & half rests below and count aloud evenly.
3. Say the finger numbers aloud while playing them in the air.
4. Play and say the finger numbers.
5. Play and say the note names.
6. Play and sing the words.

Lost Teddy Bear

**61** **16 (41)**

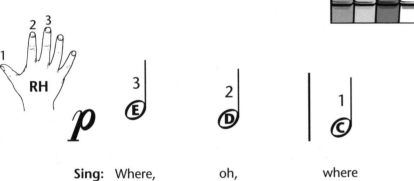

Sing:	Where,	oh,	where		is	my	bear?
Count:	1	2	1	2	1	2	Rest	2	*etc.*

🔊 **62**

In the Magical Music Book, Mozart Mouse discovered that *The C Song* also could be played with the LEFT HAND.

"Oh, certainly we should name the new version *The C Song, Again!*" he chuckled.

1 Clap (or tap) *The C Song, Again!* and count aloud evenly.

2 Point to the quarter notes & quarter rests below and count aloud evenly.

3 Using LH finger 1, play and sing the words.

The C Song, Again!

🔊 **63** 💾 **17 (42)**

Sing: C,   C,   can   it   be?   My   *left*   thumb   can   play   a   C!

Student plays one octave higher with duet.

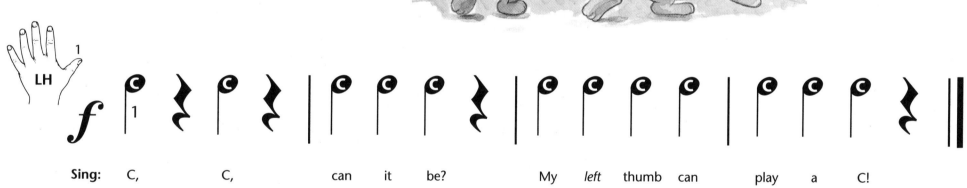

Teacher or Parent

Moving along

mf

Finding B on the Keyboard

♦64 "**W**hat key is this?" Mozart Mouse wondered.

"Oh my, I haven't learned that key yet! Let's look in the Magical Music Book to find out!" said Beethoven Bear. They looked in the book and learned that B is to the right of the **3** black keys.

1 Find each B on the keyboard below and color it PURPLE.

2 Place Beethoven Bear on your piano, touching a B.

3 Play every B on your piano keyboard.

65 "**K**ey number four! We are learning more and more!" shouted Beethoven Bear and Mozart Mouse at the same time.

They were making so much noise in their excitement that they could be heard well outside the Music Room.

1 Clap (or tap) *The B Song* and count aloud evenly.

2 Point to the quarter notes & rests below and count aloud evenly.

3 Using LH finger 2, play and sing the words.

LH
B
2

The B Song

66 18(43)

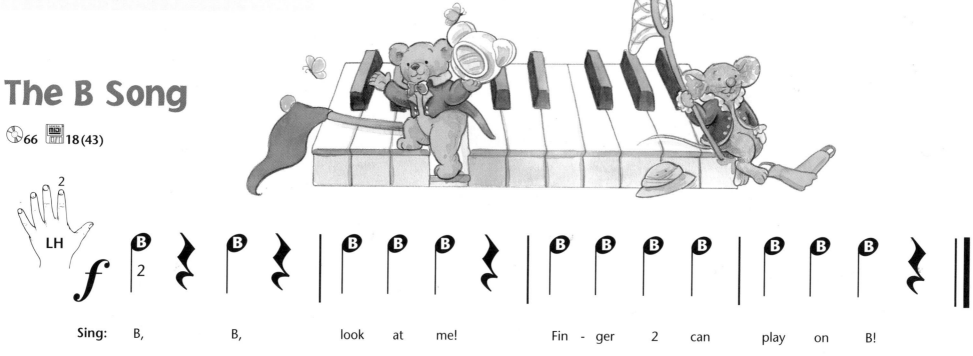

Sing: B,   B,   look at me!   Fin - ger 2 can play on B!

Relaxed (♫ = ♩♪) Student plays one octave higher with duet.

Teacher or Parent

🔘67

Around the corner, their friend, Elgar E. Elephant, heard the commotion and peered into the Music Room to investigate.

"My, my, *my*, but you two are becoming *quite* the musicians."

"Play me a song, I say! Play me MY song!"

1 Clap (or tap) *The Elephant Song* and count aloud evenly.

2 Point to the quarter notes & rests below and count aloud evenly.

3 Say the finger numbers aloud while playing them in the air.

4 Play and say the finger numbers.

5 Play and say the note names.

6 Play and sing the words.

The Elephant Song

🔘68 📟19(44)

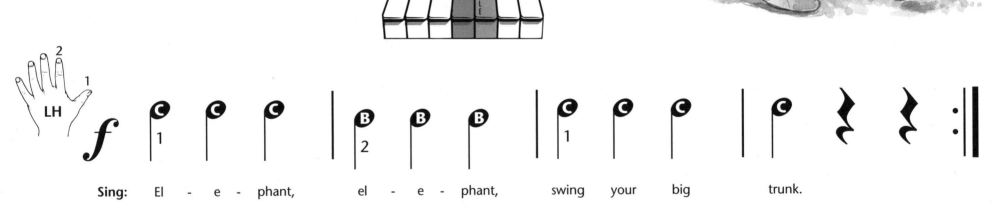

Sing: El - e - phant,   el - e - phant,   swing your big trunk.

Whole Note

🔊69 "**I** heard something about whole notes once," said Elgar E. Elephant. "Have you learned about them yet?" he asked as he went on his merry way.

Turning to Mozart Mouse, Beethoven Bear whispered, "Quick! Look in the Magical Music Book and find out what a whole note is!"

While looking, Mozart Mouse noticed a song in the Magical Music Book about nighttime, the moon and *Bright Stars*.

Bright Stars

🔊70 🎹20 (45)

1. Clap (or tap) *Bright Stars* and count aloud evenly.
2. Point to the notes below and count aloud evenly.
3. Say the finger numbers aloud while playing them in the air.
4. Play and say the finger numbers.
5. Play and say the note names.
6. Play and sing the words.

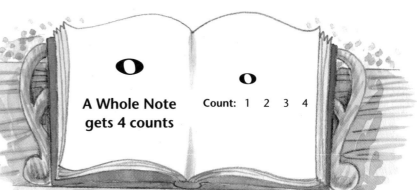

A Whole Note gets 4 counts   Count: 1 2 3 4

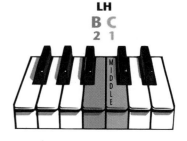

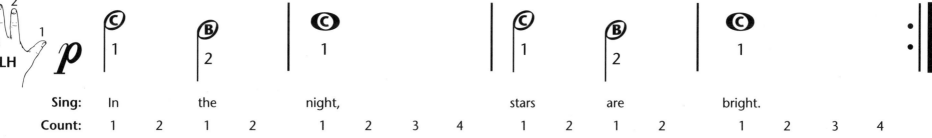

Sing: In the night, stars are bright.
Count: 1 2 1 2 1 2 3 4 1 2 1 2 1 2 3 4

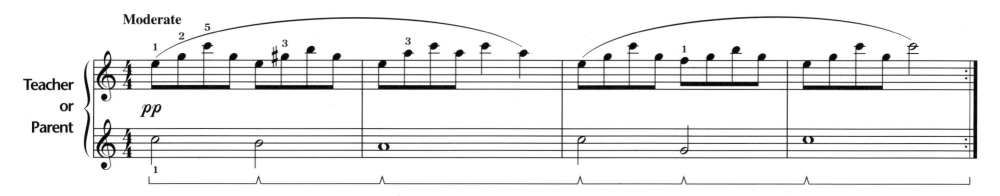

Finding A
on the Keyboard

🔘71

 "If only we could find A, then we would know our A, B, C's!" exclaimed Beethoven Bear.

 "Well, we certainly have a good start!" Mozart Mouse responded.

 Looking in the Magical Music Book, they found that A is the white key to the left of B.

1 Find each A on the keyboard below and color it BLUE.

2 Place Beethoven Bear on your piano, touching an A.

3 Play every A on your piano keyboard.

🔘72

Since Beethoven Bear and Mozart Mouse had played songs using B, C, D and E, they were now quite experienced with learning new notes.

"Do you want to play a song with A now?" Mozart Mouse started to ask.

But he didn't finish the question, because Beethoven Bear already had started to play *The A Song*.

1. Clap (or tap) *The A Song* and count aloud evenly.

2. Point to the quarter notes & rests below and count aloud evenly.

3. Using LH finger 3, play and sing the words.

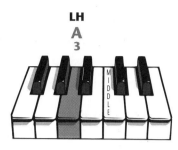

The A Song

🔘73 MIDI 21 (46)

Sing: A,   A,   hap - py   day!   Fin - ger   3   can   play   on   A!

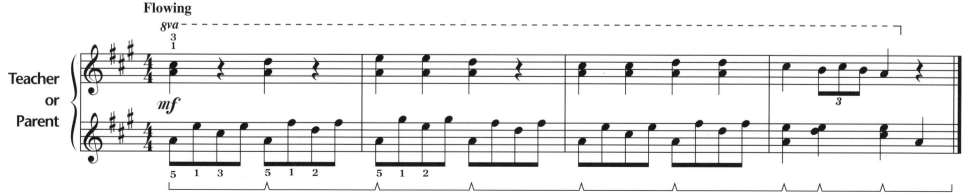

Teacher or Parent

44

74

Mozart Mouse and Beethoven Bear played the piano as often as possible, come rain or come shine.

"Beethoven Bear," said Mozart Mouse one rainy day, "we should play a song to accompany the sound of the rain. After all, the rain *is* quite rhythmic."

1. Clap (or tap) *Rainy Day* and count aloud evenly.
2. Point to the notes below and count aloud evenly.
3. Say the finger numbers aloud while playing them in the air.
4. Play and say the finger numbers.
5. Play and say the note names.
6. Play and sing the words.

Rainy Day

75 22 (47)

p C C C C | B B B B | A A A A | A ‖

| Sing: | Play | - | ing | with | our | mu | - | sic | friends | on | such | a | rain | - | y | day. |

Count: 1 1 1 1 1 1 1 1 1 1 1 1 2 3 4

Lightly
Both hands one octave higher than written

Teacher or Parent

45

Whole Rest

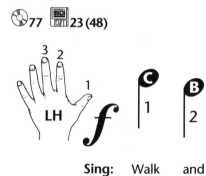

🔊76   **M**ore excited by the minute, Beethoven Bear began to dance to the music.

"Make it quick, my friend," Mozart Mouse suggested, "before the rain stops."

Strangely, on this particular day the rain would fall for four counts, then stop for four counts. Beethoven Bear creatively did the same. Oh, it was a beautiful dance!

1. Clap (or tap) *Little Dance* and count aloud evenly.
2. Point to the notes below and count aloud evenly.
3. Say the finger numbers aloud while playing them in the air.
4. Play and say the finger numbers.
5. Play and say the note names.
6. Play and sing the words.

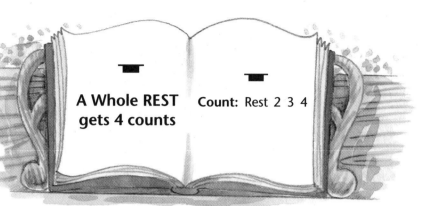

A Whole REST gets 4 counts   Count: Rest 2 3 4

Little Dance

🔊77 💾23 (48)

Sing:	Walk	and	stop.				Walk	and	stop.			
Count:	1	1	1 2	Rest	2	3 4	1	1	1 2	Rest	2	3 4

Delicately
Both hands one octave higher than written

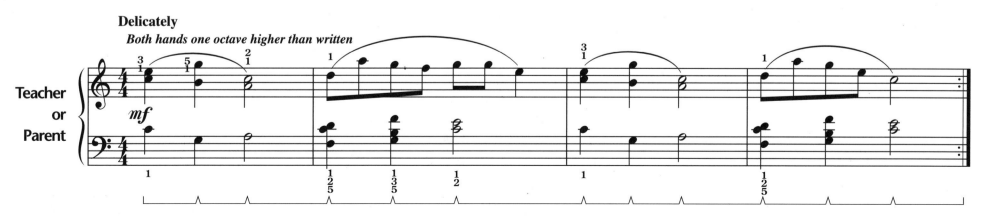

Teacher or Parent

78

After many happy days at the piano, Beethoven Bear had an idea. "I know!" he cried. "Let's have a concert and invite our friends! We can play the music we've written!"

"That's a wonderful idea!" piped in Mozart Mouse. "We will need to go to bed early to make sure that we get plenty of rest for our very first music concert."

1 Clap (or tap) *Off to Bed* and count aloud evenly.

2 Point to the notes & rests and count aloud evenly.

3 Say the finger numbers aloud while playing them in the air.

4 Play and say the finger numbers.

5 Play and say the note names.

6 Play and sing the words.

MIDDLE C POSITION for LH

Off to Bed

79 24(49)

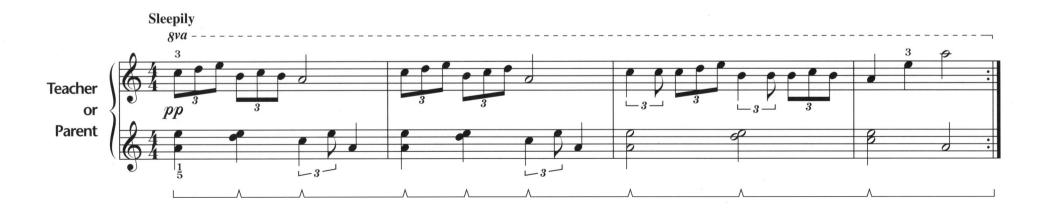

🔊80 The day of the concert was clear and bright. Beethoven Bear and Mozart Mouse put on their finest concert clothes.

The Music Room was filled with all their toy friends. When it was time for Beethoven Bear and Mozart Mouse to perform, they weren't scared. They had practiced so well that they played all of their pieces beautifully!

① Clap (or tap) *Concert Day* and count aloud evenly.

② Point to the notes & rests and count aloud evenly.

③ Say the finger numbers aloud while playing them in the air.

④ Play and say the finger numbers.

⑤ Play and say the note names.

⑥ Play and sing the words.

MIDDLE C POSITION for RH

Concert Day

🔊81 📟 25 (50)

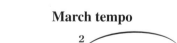

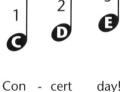

| Sing: | Shout | "hoo | - ray!" | | Con | - cert | day! | | Time | | to | | play! | | |
| Count: | 1 | 1 | 1 | Rest | 1 | 1 | 1 | Rest | 1 | 2 | 1 | 2 | 1 | 2 | 3 | 4 |

March tempo

Teacher or Parent

mf

LH detached

8va- - - - - -

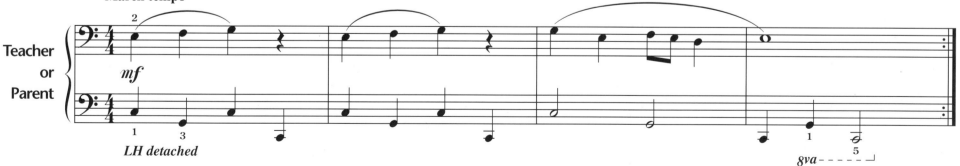

🔊82

When the concert ended, all of their friends stood up and cheered. "Bravo, Bravo!" they cried. As Beethoven Bear and Mozart Mouse were taking one last bow, they looked up and were surprised to see that the children of the house were standing there and clapping, too! Beethoven Bear and Mozart Mouse did not know what to do! They had been caught in the Music Room!

"Don't be afraid," the children said, "We came to get books for our piano lesson and were so surprised to discover that you could play! Would you like to come with us to our piano lesson and learn more about music?"

Beethoven Bear and Mozart Mouse looked at each other in amazement. Who wouldn't want to take piano lessons? They eagerly climbed inside the children's music bags and went out the door with them to their lesson.

YOU too can join Beethoven Bear, Mozart Mouse and the children at their piano lessons. Continue your musical adventure with our music friends in *Music for Little Mozarts*, Book 2.

Beethoven Bear, Mozart Mouse and the Children hereby invite

✗ _____

to join them for
Piano Lessons in
Music for Little Mozarts, Book 2

RSVP to
_____
Teacher